Brown Eyes

Isa Gene

authorHOUSE®

AuthorHouse™ UK Ltd.
500 Avebury Boulevard
Central Milton Keynes, MK9 2BE
www.authorhouse.co.uk
Phone: 08001974150

First published by AuthorHouse 5/25/2010

ISBN: 978-1-4490-8393-9 (sc)

This book is printed on acid-free paper.

This book is written to celebrate the life of a faithful companion and to be a perpetual memory of his life.

This book is dedicated to my dear friend Sue, without whom the book would never have been written.

I thank all Nutty's many friends both canine and human for the part they played in his life and especially Nichole for the loving attention she gave him.

Chapter 1

A bandoned: At six years old, along with my blanket and toys, I have been dumped. The packing must have been done in secret, probably whilst I was out playing in the garden as I had no inkling of this coming event. I was only told that we were going to visit Auntie Sue, so willingly I jumped in the car, got strapped into the back seat, and we were off. I watched the passing scenery and felt the familiar tremble of excitement as we neared our destination; I am fond of Auntie Sue. It is not a long journey and is one I am very familiar with so within the hour we are pulling into the driveway. Pleased to see us, Auntie Sue greets us at the door making a particularly big fuss of me and I was taken into the kitchen and given a drink and a biscuit, having thus satisfied my immediate needs I looked around to re-locate my special person, but she has disappeared. I rush around the house searching for her but she was not to be found anywhere and I was distressed. I was kissed and cuddled but I cried and sulked and would not be comforted. My exclusive important person had gone, the one I loved and by whom I was loved in return and was secure in that love, believing that I was as important to her as she was to me. Perhaps I was wrong; what I wondered had precipitated this abrupt departure? But I have started my story in the middle; let me recap and introduce myself. I was born in Lincoln; my mother's name was Muffin, I never knew my father but I believe he was from the Sandringham estate in Norfolk, I like to think I have royal blood in my veins and have developed a proud manner and practiced a haughty look. (Perhaps this is what drove her away, I hope not as I desperately need her back.) At home there were several siblings we had a large garden and we spent a lot of our time in noisy boisterous play, racing around on the grass and staging mock fights. We had no cares in our secure world, our Mother looked after us well, occasionally scolding us when we got too rough but we were happy and care free, and we never gave our absent Father so much as a passing thought. Sometimes we had visitors who were interested in seeing us and one day a lady came to our house who was quite taken by me, she gazed into my liquid brown eyes and was lost. I squirmed in her arms and quivered with longing and anticipation, she said I was quite nutty, so Nutty, I became and I was hers. Thus I was separated from the litter of pups and my new life began. I am a Chocolate Labrador and my pedigree name is Winter Walnut; rather a regal name don't you think? I went home with my new mistress and we became inseparable, we were happy together, but at times I fear she found me very hard work; I admit I was quite a handful with an irrepressible nature and boundless energy and I was rather mischievous. Looking back I realise now just what a difficult and destructive youngster I had been, indeed had the government come up with the Antisocial Behaviour Orders scheme back then, I expect I would have been served with a few. But I managed to get through my youth without a criminal record, although I did have some stern official warnings from the mistress.

Chapter 2

$\mathcal{A}$t my old home where I was born I was kept within a small area with access to the garden, but here in my new abode I had free range of both the house and the garden. I was able to be with my new mistress most of the time and she delighted in playing with me and watching my antics. She provided me with toys and sat on the floor to play with me and took me out into the garden with her for more energetic games. We went out on walks and I got to know this new area, she also taught me to walk on a lead and got me used to wearing a harness for when I went in the car. There was so much to learn and so much to explore, and a lot of the exploring I did with my teeth. I now have a track record that some with a long memory can recall and appear to enjoy recounting my misdeeds. The problems were not all my fault, we were on different wavelengths and she failed to understand my need to express myself as only a new Labrador puppy can, I loved my new mistress but there was a long battle of wits, I was striving to be top dog, whilst she was determined to get the master of me and be the pack leader. I was also coping with the trauma of being severed from my mother, my family and my safe environment and taking a long time to adjust. Despite all that, I found my new environment thrilling and explored every crook and cranny, finding things to chew everywhere I looked. I chewed anything that was left within my reach, I just had to have something in my mouth so would pick up whatever was handy and race around the house with it. I stole the washing from the basket and dragged it out into the garden and having grown bored with it, left it out in the mud. When the mistress was getting dressed I would grab the end of the garment she was putting on and tug and pull at it to try and get it off her, then I would pick up a shoe and race off with it; it was all such fun and she seemed to enjoy it too for she would laugh.

There was always something that attracted my attention when we went out, some new thing to see or enticing smells to put my nose to, I liked being out with her we met new people and I got extra attention. She also took me in the car with her for short rides to get me used to travelling. Indoors I would follow her about the house watching everything she did and sometimes joining in, we had great games when she was doing the housework; the vacuum cleaner would steal my toys and she would hold them up in the air for me to leap up and snatch back, then I would race round with it in my mouth and she would chase me as I scampered up and down the stairs, panting with excitement. Sometimes she would go out and leave me indoors, in the conservatory; I did not care for being on my own for I very soon became bored and lonely and frustrated. I much preferred to have people to talk to me and make a fuss of me, however being left alone did have compensations for I was able to indulge in serious chewing without being disturbed.

One day that I recall, a workman came to carry out some repairs to our house, he was to do some work with a drain under the floor of the conservatory. I watched him as he meticulously rolled back the Vinyl flooring carried out the necessary work and then very carefully re-laid it. I was fascinated to see this as I had not known that this was possible and I thought to myself, I could do that, and that night I did. It was a struggle and it took me a long time but perseverance won through. It kept me occupied for many hours whilst the mistress was sleeping. I had some problem getting the vinyl up as there was a lot of it, but I was eventually successful in my efforts to remove it; I just ripped it to shreds.

On another of my lonely night vigils, looking for some entertainment and being bored with sleep I was prowling around my confined space to see what I could find to distract me when I came across a snake-like object coiled up behind the freezer. I pounced, I attacked it with vigour before it could get either my Mistress or me; I killed it, biting it in half. My Mistress was not pleased when she found out in the morning, in fact she was rather alarmed at the danger I had been in, but somehow or other this thing was important to her in keeping the freezer at the right temperature so my efforts were unwanted and I was severely scolded. She replaced it with a new one. I did not appreciate this adverse reaction to my brave efforts at protection, so a few weeks later I ambushed it once more and slaughtered it.

Once more left to my own devices when she went out I found behind the washing machine another strange object, thick squidgy and mobile it looked just the thing to test out my sharp teeth. It took a lot of chewing but I severed it, unfortunately when I did it retaliated by throwing water over me. I retreated to a safe distance and watched in horror whilst the water poured out and spread over the floor. Fortunately my Mistress returned before the water level reached my face or I might have drowned. I was given a good brisk rub with a towel to restore me to my pristine condition (in addition to a good scolding.)

I have been left again, shut in this room, off she went shopping, how I hate that word for I am never invited along, I am always left behind, she had taken me for a walk before she left but the pleasure of that was long gone. I am shut in the conservatory; so once again I am bored and looking for entertainment, I seem to have explored everything there is in this space. My body is bursting with suppressed energy and my mind is in need of stimulation; outside the sun is shining and I can hear the birds singing and pattering about on the roof, next doors cat is mewling in the vicinity as well, probably invading my territory. I look longingly out and wish for a playmate. Idling my time away standing with my paws up on the windowsill to watch the birds, I caught my claw in the net curtains and when I pulled it away, the curtain wire stretched and retracted. Fascinated I tried again. Good game! This looked like a new and exciting past time. I race around the room, plenty of curtains here, I bunch them up into my jaws, I bite and growl, pull and tug and gradually they begin to tear and I get them onto the floor for a good tussle of strength, shaking them vigorously too and fro, it quite made my head spin. I was able to spend the rest of the afternoon engaged with this new enemy so by the time I had them all down and shredded I was quite weary, so I heaped them up in a corner making myself a comfortable soft bed and settled for a quiet snooze, a job well done. There I was at peace enjoying a quiet rest dreaming of the sort of things doggies dream of; but, there is always a BUT! The quietness did not last long when SHE came home!

I was not always confined to the conservatory; sometimes I went with her in the car, I liked travelling around to new places, we visited friends who treated me with great respect and made me welcome or we went into the countryside and found new walks through woods or beside the river and on occasion, to the beach. I liked watching out of the car window with my head stuck out and my ears flapping in the wind; so many enticing smells whipped by making my nose twitch. If the journey was long and I got a bit bored I would look for entertainment inside the car to while away the time, there was usually something around to chew even if it was only the seat belts which I demolished bit by bit. When we were at home I followed her around the house and garden and generally tried to be a helpful boy. I could equal anything that she did. We have a large garden that takes up much of her time, there is a noisy machine that she pushes over the grass, I like this and I always insist that she plays football with me as she goes up and down. I would watch where she put the new plants and then when she wasn't looking I would dig them up. Sneaking up behind her I would steal the plant pots and race round the garden with them, she would laugh and took to throwing them for me when she had finished with them (even now I am partial to chewing up plant pots, I like to crush them in my jaws and make crunchy noises.) I also managed to make a large hole in the garden fence so that I could spy on the neighbours. I took to escaping through this bolt hole and this worried my mistress to distraction but it served her right, now she knew what mental trauma I suffer when she leaves me. I always returned with a trophy, one day a box of matches another day a flat cap, on another occasion I brought her a live toad and dropped it in the kitchen. My best trophy was a plastic duck I pinched from someone's pond. I loved that duck and kept it many years.

(An aside from the mistress: I had visions of Nutty creeping up behind some little old man in his garden, who sitting for a rest on his bench seat would place his belongings beside him only to have this sneaky thief come up from behind and purloin them! I never did find out where he went on these escapades. It is amazing what he can carry in his soft mouth without damaging it and sometimes he carries things quite hidden for ages before he will drop it.)

New fencing was erected to keep me in but I still managed to squeeze through the gaps between the roots of the hedge on the opposite side so she was never able to keep tabs on me except when I was indoors helping her with the housework. I liked to have my toys (and I had a lot) scattered into every room, it gave me a feeling of belonging and of possession. I used them to stake a claim on my space, when she tidied them away I spread them around again. In the evenings I lay at the feet of my mistress whilst she read her book or did paperwork and she would praise me for being a good boy, not realising that what was keeping me quiet was my secret nibbling of the wall paper or carpet or anything she had been stupid enough to leave within my reach. Despite these escapades and subsequent scolding we enjoyed each other, and as the weeks and months went by and we were well into our routine.

As the year passes the weather is getting colder now and walks are sometimes wet ones. I like cold windy weather, the cold invigorates me and the wind makes me frisky, bringing new smells drifting up my nostrils. I kick up my heels like the horses in the field and race off in front then turn and race back as she holds out her arms pretending to catch me, but I dodge and race off again. I like the frost when the air is clean and fresh and we walk briskly to stave off the cold and come back warm and glowing for a refreshing drink and a titbit. When the leaves are falling off the trees and carpeting the grass the mistress likes to shuffle her feet through them making noises and pushing them into clumps. I like to snuffle my nose in them as they are full of musty smells.

At home there has been a lot of activity and visitors are expected, preparations are made as Christmas approaches, lots of extra shopping trips and exciting packages come into the house. Pete is here for a few days; I like Pete and he likes me because he takes me for extra long and interesting walks on which there are new things to grab my attention. Before leaving us again he brought the decorations and the tree down from the loft space and left them in the conservatory ready for my mistress to put up. She never did erect and decorate that tree; that night I trashed it; she was very cross. I could sense that her patience was becoming sorely tried and shortly after this a large sleeping cage appeared in the conservatory where I was put to sleep every night. After that, I was very pleased to see my mistress in the morning or when she came home and she was pleased to see me. I must have been forgiven for when Christmas came I had my own stocking bulging with new toys and treats (this despite me barking furiously at Father Christmas when he called with his collection tin.) The family have arrived for the seasonal celebrations and we are all very jolly, I am being made to wear a paper hat around my neck, but I don't mind as there is lots of activity and extra special treats. One of my gifts was a Giggly ball, which is great fun to push around. I romp around all over with it banging into furniture and pushing it with paw and snout so that it giggles. I particularly like doing this when she is on the phone which she finds annoying but if she has time to chat she has time to play.

An aside from the mistress: (Christmas with Nutty is always a source of delight and merriment, whenever bulging shopping bags begin to appear in the house, Nutty is in there. Head thrust firmly into each bag he explores the parcels, he is particularly fond of anything that is soft and cuddly or makes a noise, he is not averse to stealing one if he can manage it. I take parcels and packages into the spare bedroom to wrap in secret; he hears every rustle of paper and comes in at speed, ears pricked eyes bright tail out ready for the search. His questing nose seems able to pick out any that are for him and if it happens to be a noisy one his curiosity knows no bounds. He is very good once the parcels are wrapped and placed under the tree he will inspect them daily but never takes them. On Christmas morning he burrows his head deep into his stocking and pulls out all the goodies, then he comes to help anyone else who is showing les ability to get the paper off their presents. He rips and tears in great excitement until there is nothing else left to open, only then is it time to get inside the packets for a snack.)

I don't know why SHE keeps butting into my story for I am quite capable of recalling all the incidents in my life for I have a good memory and am a good story teller. Spring is here and a large outdoor pen and smart kennel have been erected in the garden, I now go in there when the mistress goes out. I am still entertained with chewing and strewing my bedding over the pen. The mistress is hard put to keep me in dry bedding as I constantly drag it outside and leave it in the rain. Uncle John came up with the idea of getting a large pallet and nailing a piece of carpet to it and putting this in the kennel for me to sleep on. In came a large wooden pallet, out came the nails and she hammered the carpet firmly down, then into the kennel it went. By the time she came back in the afternoon, the carpet was ripped up and left outside. Out came the hammer, more nails and a larger piece of carpet; wrapped all around the pallet the carpet was nailed firmly on both sides. I still got it off. She tried tying raggies and balls on ropes to the wire cage for me to play with and keep me occupied but I found it much more challenging and entertaining to undo her good work! In the end she gave up the battle. I was particularly fond of chewing tough hairy doormats and this obsession stayed with me for many years though she tried to dissuade me from this activity. Admitting defeat, she bought me a new one every week having found a cheap and easy source of them.

The mistress again! Over the years I have spent a small fortune on beds; wanting only his absolute comfort I have researched different types in various materials and styles. One year I purchased a large and expensive beanbag for him to stretch out on thinking he could relax in style; I thought he would appreciate it but he would not lie on it. It spent weeks in the lounge, I sat on it and tried my best to coax him and even tried to push and pull him onto it; he would have none of it, pitting his pulling power against mine and he won. Was it the noise of the beans shifting or perhaps the movement? I will never know, suffice it to say Nutty would go nowhere near it and it was eventually given away. Now he just has a fleece blanket on the floor and appears happy with that. Even now if he thinks I have been out past my allotted time he will drag his blanket out into the garden and leave it there, he seems to think this is punishing me!

Despite my early mistakes, I grew up to be a fine dog, though my mistress still tells other people that I did not start to grow brain cells until I was two and then it was a slow process. A rather hurtful remark really. She tried taking me to puppy training classes but at that time in my life I was not ready for advanced learning; too full of exuberance and the joy of living I just wanted to play with the other dogs. She had enrolled us on a seriously upmarket class as obviously she thought that only the best was good enough for me. I was eventually expelled from this exclusive training school for not paying attention; she was very put out when the lady in charge said in her loud imperative voice in front of all the others in the group,

"I would rather you did not bring him to this class."

She slunk off in disgrace with her head down taking me with her, after that she accepted me for what I was and left me to develop at my own pace. We had a constant battle for the place of top dog, I thought it should be me and she obviously had a different view. In the end we compromised, I have learned obedience and will obey commands but I rule the roost most of the time, I have both her and Auntie Sue wrapped around my paw and organise them to my satisfaction, however when I meet with aggression from some other dog when we are out, I tuck myself safely behind her legs and let her deal with it! I also do this when any large vehicle thunders down the road, I prefer not to be on the nearside. I have been particularly nervous of this since a trailer being pulled by a passing tractor swung out and clipped me, knocking me in the ditch.

Chapter 3

*T*here are many events in my life I could tell you about and having observed human behaviour when they meet, everyone asks after the other person's wellbeing, so I may as well tell you about my health. Within the first year of my life I had to have operations on my ears and was made to wear a lampshade round my neck for several weeks, how stupid I felt and how difficult it was to get through the door. As if this was not enough I began to suffer from problems in my joints which seriously affected my ability to walk. Realising that I had a problem I was taken to the Vet and following tests this was diagnosed as Arthritis. I was by now limping on a front leg and dragging a back leg and I found it difficult to get in and out the car; I was no longer the exuberant puppy I should have been. I was too young to be afflicted in this way and my Mistress sought out treatments from the vet and other sources, injections, pills and potions to no avail. Rescue from this debilitating disease came from one of my friends at the kennels; yes I did say kennels where SHE would occasionally leave me and disappear. Fortunately being a friendly chap with an appealing nature I was popular there so did not mind too much. One of the kennel owners showed my mistress an advert for a new special food; this was sent for and it brought about a great change to my life, giving me back my active puppyhood. Within weeks I began to perk up, my coat was shiny and I was able to run and jump about just as before. My mistress was so delighted she wrote to thank the manufacturers to say so, even telling them she might try it in a cereal bowl with milk on in the morning to see if it would do the same for her! So pleased were they to receive this letter, they promptly sent a photographer down to take my picture. I came to fame overnight, appearing in the advertising brochure and receiving as my reward free food for a year which suited me fine as I was and still am, fond of eating.

I was a popular sight in the neighbourhood, when we went out walking everyone stopped to pet me. They would feed my ego by complimenting me on my good looks. I was told I had a noble head; (this must come through my royal sire.) Outings brought new exhilarating experiences. I would Hoover up anything on the ground including pebbles I then had the indignity of having my mouth prized open and my head shaken until I dropped them all. Out with

Auntie Sue on one occasion this strange behaviour was observed by a drunken Irishman, who asked her what she was doing, she demonstrated and I dropped the pebbles.

"I'll give you fifty pounds for him." said he.

Auntie Sue was well and truly insulted on my behalf and told him in no uncertain terms my true value, not that she would have parted with me for any price. I was very observant when I went out, noticing all the cats hiding beneath parked cars and chasing anything that moved; I especially liked to get the scent of a rabbit, nose down, tail up I would track it, sometimes flushing it out and giving chase, but I never caught it. I was made to leave the birds in the garden alone, our garden is a haven for birds and at times they even have the temerity to fly into my conservatory; when this happens I fetch the mistress and she catches them and sets them free. (Those cheeky Blackbirds in my garden seemed to know I was under orders to leave them alone, so they invade my space hopping about near me all the time whilst I am trying to have a quiet snooze and pulling out the plants from the tubs, something I would not dare do!) But down on the riverbanks I chase all the ducks off the bank into the water and like to hear the noisy indignation they make. I soon learned to swim and could follow them out in the river for a while. Those ducks cheat; when I swim after them they take to the air and fly further down stream, but I have their measure, I get out on the opposite side, run down the bank and get back into the water behind them again.

Life is full of surprises and one sunny day I recall taking my mistress for a stroll and saw an amazing sight. Two strange objects came floating down the river and each of these things was being propelled along by a human being with a stick. I had never seen anything like it; what were they doing? With bounding energy and enthusiasm I raced too and fro on the bank barking then I stood dumbfounded and quivering with excitement whilst they watched me and laughed at my antics. I could contain myself no longer and with one flying leap I launched myself off the bank landing on top of one of them; that soon put paid to their laughter. Whilst I clambered out and shook myself all over the mistress the lady in the canoe struggled to keep afloat as I had almost caused it to overturn. When she had settled herself on a steady course she enquired about my name and on being told this, agreed that Nutty was a very good name for such as me.

Chapter 4

*M*y mistress has a daughter who owns two Border Collies; we meet sometimes on the riverbank and expend much energy in playful rivalry. Although the adults do not want us playing with sticks we like them, Freddie is good at finding sticks and I am good at pinching them from him, so we argue and play tug of war, knocking over anybody who gets in our way. The smaller one, Fly a quarrelsome female, refuses to join in our play but lends to the atmosphere by constantly barking. When the game gets too hot we swim, still hanging grimly on to our own end of the stick. Fly shows her disapproval by giving us crafty nips as we clamber out, she is a real spoilsport. One of these bites I got resulted in a trip to the vet, it was Freddie who did it because he was peeved at me for taking the stick. I like collecting plastic bottles from the reeds that fishermen have left behind, they make crunchy noises when chewed. It is also fun crashing about in the reeds flushing out all the ducks and sending them quacking, and I am entertained by the coots having a domestic and scooting across the water chasing after each other. Freddie and Fly sometimes come to stay at my house, I am not keen on having them as it means I have to share my mistress; I am given to sulking on these occasions. My old sleeping cage is brought out for Fly, as she still chews when she is anxious. When bedtime comes I am first in the cage; after all it is MINE, Fly follows and we get locked in together for the night. Freddie will sleep on the furniture if he can, so cushions are removed and the chairs tipped to prevent this, he has a blanket on the floor.

I keep referring to walks but really these are the highlight of the day for we both love to be out in the fresh air and most of our adventures happen when we are out. Whatever the weather we stride out to see who we can meet and what we can see. Rain does not deter me but Auntie Sue tells me she doesn't do wet walks however she realises that my comfort is far more important than hers so she does take me out. The mistress doesn't seem to mind too much though the distance we go is usually cut short. She puts on a stout raincoat with a hood and off we go; we don't meet many other dog walkers out! We do see frogs having a swim in the puddles and usually large slugs and worms are out on the road so obviously they like the wet. I get a good rub down on my return home. Even better are the crisp frosty days, everyone is wrapped up against the cold and I have got my thick winter coat on so the cold doesn't penetrate. Our breath is like a cloud in the air before us and we walk fast or even run part of the way to stir up the blood and produce some heat. Summer evenings by the river are my favourite for we seem to stay out for an extra long time; the mistress will stroll slowly along watching the water and looking out for the kingfisher and the herons or if it is dusk, for the owl that hunts along the bank. Me I keep a wary eye on the swans who are never very pleased to see me, they hiss and glare in an intimidating manner and chatter their beaks at me. Discretion being the better part of valour, I give them a wide berth as I jump in and out of the water to cool off. These waters are breeding grounds for frogs and the mistress often stops to peer at one of the changelings crawling through the grass, but I find them boring, real frogs are better besides I find the many mole hills much more worthy of investigating, I always stop for a good sniff at these. One day we saw a fox on the opposite bank, he was harassing a duck that had a nest of chicks in the reeds. That duck was squawking and quacking fit to bust, swimming in circles and flapping her wings. The fox spied us and we stood and eyed him for ages, all of us staring at the other; eventually that fox slunk off so we had done our good deed for the day, but poor old foxy lost his dinner.

Auntie Sue lives near the woods and we combine a walk with a visit to her. The woods are interesting for there are lots of animal smells for me to explore; sometimes we see a lone deer in the distance but recently a herd of deer crossed over the path in front of us; I kept very still. There are burrows and holes to sniff at, but I don't know who lives in them, but squirrels jump out all over the place and these are good to chase. When I meet other dogs we like to greet each other and will play and chase for as long as we are allowed. Recently we met two other Chocolate Labradors, I am always ecstatic to meet up with my own kind. Beside myself with joy I run up the path come back at full speed and jump over both of them, they just stood and looked up at me as I flew over. Astonished by this behaviour the owner asked how old I was as his dogs did not have my energy and ability, older than both of them put together, but they were so fat, they could hardly move! They were certainly missing out on the joy of life, my mistress would never have allowed me to overeat and get like that. We head for home tired but refreshed and then it is time for dinner and a well earned rest at the mistress's feet. I like this too, both of us close and at peace with the world and each other.

The mistress again: *Auntie Sue lives near the woods and we combine walks there with a visit to her. Ever since he was left for a few days with Sue, Nutty keeps a wary eye on both of us; he will not go into the house until he makes sure I am close behind! Once he has been offered refreshment he will lie down and allow us an hour for tea and chat and then he begins to fidget he doesn't want to be left and makes it plain that he is anxious to go home. As Sue says, it's a good job she is not sensitive!*

Chapter 5

*T*here is much activity at home, apparently we are moving house. All our possessions are being packed away into boxes; needless to say I have to play a part in this. I have my head in every box to check the contents and although this is exciting it worries me somewhat as well. I feel very insecure and wonder what is going on for I hate my routine upset, but in the end all is well, we have moved to a bungalow that has a secure garden and new territory to explore. The mistress is busy putting all our things in place and very soon it all looks familiar once more, though the conservatory where I am to sleep is somewhat inferior to what I have been used to. I soon discovered that that there were two other Chocolate Labradors in the area we meet on our walks down the lane, our owners compare notes whilst we play and chase each other over the fields. This lane is a popular spot for dog walking so I meet many canine friends, all shapes and sizes, large and small, some only as big as an animated teddy bear, but they are all interested in stopping for a sniff and a play. I have a very active fan club, the children in the street all stop their play to greet me, and acquaintances of my mistress all pet me and make a fuss of me and on occasion give me titbits. We go visiting friends and I am always made welcome. Sometimes I go in the car with my Mistress to work or night school, of course I remain in the car most of the time but there are breaks for nice walks and the window is left open so I can keep tabs on what goes on outside. One place she visits is a residential home, I like that as there are a lot of people to fuss me and I can normally cajole a snack or two when SHE is not looking! In fact they usually have a biscuit or two in their handbag in readiness for my visit. These occasions are always in the winter as in the summer is too hot to stay in the car and there are built in stops for my exercise and comfort.

I am king of the garden. I patrol it many times a day but it is visited by many other small creatures and birds. One evening I found a strange animal on the lawn so barked to alert my mistress to this invasion. I do not bark often so she knows it is something she should follow up; strangely she seemed to be delighted to see this hedgehog as she called it and bid me leave it alone. I would have done anyway as it prickled my nose when I tried to investigate it.

Note from the mistress; Nutty only barks when something either startles him or is new to his experience. He has a rich deep bark that takes one by surprise because of its rarity, when he was a puppy he barked at some friends who poked their heads over the fence wearing helmets and goggles but after that just accepted such sights. I recall an occasion when we were walking on a lonely riverbank and a solitary male walked towards us; Nutty ran forward and stood foursquare in front of him, barking; the man veered off and gave us a wide berth. He did it once when he was out with Sue in the park and a noisy group of overgrown boys spilled out of the pub and took over the path jostling and pushing at each other. Sue stopped and Nutty stretched out as far as the lead would reach and gave vent to his disapproval. Having asked if he would bite and being told he would, they apologised to Sue and took the opposite direction! What made him react like this, is it his protective instinct, does he sense some unease in his handler or was he picking up vibes from the other people? We shall never know but it is reassuring to know that he can divert unwanted attention, though I am sure he would never ever bite as there is no aggression in him.

That winter a baby hedgehog came to stay for a while. We found it cold and hungry in the frost and it was brought into the kitchen and given tinned DOG food! I did not approve of this even though it was a tin left behind by Freddie, as I always have the dried food. My old sleeping cage was erected in the conservatory and this creature was placed inside, I gave vent to hearty disapproval at this betrayal, besides it didn't do much good as it could get through the bars, so it lived in a box in the kitchen. When the grandchildren came to stay they found it interesting and named it Holly, It stayed for some time and my mistress seemed to be fascinated as she watched it grow and keep escaping from its box, but I was happier when it left as I felt it was diverting attention from me. I was much more interested in the Frog that took up residence in the water tub outside; he sometimes sits on a large leaf and I watch him, quivering with anticipation I stare as I wait with my nose on the edge of the barrel for it to leap. When he does, he makes me jump too.

Chapter 6

*T*here has been another interesting development in my life, a little black puppy called Daisy has moved in next door. At times she is a bit of a pest; she visits me and even eats my dinner, and I, valiant gentleman that I am, let her! This invasion took a bit of getting used to but we quickly established a lasting friendship. We talk to each other through the fence; she is so fond of my company she used to try and dig through from her side. This left gaps under the fence where I could put one of my toys for her to pull through to her side to play with, is this love? Now she thinks she rules the roost around here, barking at everyone who calls at my house; the cheek of it! Actually it is quite a good arrangement as we look after Daisy when she is left alone and her mistress does the same for me when SHE is out. The children share their affection between Daisy and me, so that is fine. We go on long walks together; like me she is fond of chasing rabbits, so we have mutual interests. Sometimes on summer evenings we all go down the lanes, the mistresses and the children on their bikes and Daisy and I run about on the grassy edge. We are quite exhausted on our return. During one of our joint walks by the river when Daisy was a very small pup, I went for a swim and she came too near the edge to see what I was doing. Much to the alarm of the adults Daisy fell in and floundered in the cold water; but I swam round her in circles until I shepherded her into the bank so she could get out, sadly this experience put her off water for life; she doesn't know what she is missing.

Quite early in my life I got used to going for short stays at the kennels although I really did not like to be parted from my mistress but it had to be tolerated. Even when I go to Auntie Sue I show my displeasure by sulking. I do not make too much fuss but when SHE returns there is a definite coolness in my greeting and I sulk for the remainder of the evening. She has to learn that she has earned my disapproval, so I lie with my back to her instead of being in my usual place with my head on her feet. I have a very expressive back and I have perfected the skill of giving reproachful looks and deep sighs, which I know will make her feel extremely guilty. Of course this is only play-acting for eventually she raises her voice and tells me to stop sulking and get over here and sit with her; so I do. I take my responsibility at protection very seriously indeed, I am always first at the door and strangers visibly step back when my nose appears at the opening. I have a very quiet approach saving my deep bark only for something suspicious but I am very watchful and alert. In fact some people refer to me as "Neighbourhood Watch" because I know everything that goes on; I sit at the side gate and spy on everyone absorbing all that goes on in the street. If my neighbour hears me bark when the mistress is out she comes to investigate as she knows there is a stranger about, I am on guard at all times, my mistress cannot even move an ornament in the house without me inspecting it and giving it my approval. My bark is very deep and as I save it for occasional use, it startles anyone who hears it, I sound quite fierce but I'm a softie really. Talking of soft, I love soft toys sometimes I manage to sneak them from visiting children or ones the mistress has bought to give away. I have lots of them as I get new ones supplied as presents (some as a sop to her conscience when she goes away and leaves me) I really must have something to carry about and if a toy is not handy then a shoe will do. I get some very hurtful sarcastic remarks when I am seen carrying my fluffy bear around. "Killer dog" is one of their favourite hurtful remarks, they do not seem to realise that a fellow needs his Teddy. My mistress bought Uncle John a furry talking pig from both of us when he was ill, (in truth I really wanted to keep it for myself) after all John had a whole collection of pigs. Sadly he has left us now and Auntie Sue has given me one of his pigs as my very own.

Chapter 7

Nutty is a benign dictator, I am sure he practices hypnosis; fixing you with steady big brown eye, that never waver he lies with his head stretched out on his front on paws and stares until you feel uncomfortable and get up to do his bidding. He has set his own parameters and has expressive body language and various "voices" to let you know what he wants. Labradors are very food orientated so his routine revolves around food walks and sleep. He will not be ignored! Our morning walks are timed to meet "the Biscuit Lady" who carries snacks for every animal she meets, Nutty is eager to be off in the morning so that he does not miss out. There are various routes we take for walking, he decides which way we go, but morning walks never vary for fear of missing his treat.

Half an hour before bedtime he starts to fidget, when I tell him it is too soon, he slumps down with an exaggerated sigh, if I ignore him too long, he plonks himself on my lap on top of my book or paper, all five stone of him.

"You are sitting on my book mister" I tell him.

(He is known affectionately as "Mr Nutty" in deference to his regal presence and irascible ways.)

The tail wags but he looks away, eyeing me from the corners of his eyes, he will not move until I agree it is time for bed, and his bedtime biscuit! There are so many incidents to recall about Nutty; once when we were on holiday and walking down a country lane, Nutty became interested in the base of a large tree, going round and round it nose down tail up oblivious of anything else. Beyond the wire fence there was a field of curious cows that gradually approached the fence to see what was going on. Sue and I could anticipate what was going to happen as Nutty was still in the world of ecstatic smells and blissfully ignorant of the interest shown by the herd. Suddenly a large tongue snaked out and licked right up his rather exposed rear end, I have never seen a dog jump so quick or quite as high as he wheeled around to face the attacking enemy. The indignation and look of affront on his face had both Sue and I falling about in laughter. He was not amused.

He really is good at navigation though people find this hard to believe. I recall going to Sue's many years ago just after they had moved to a new town; we had only been once before and this time I went wrong. There are two roads that run almost parallel, I took the wrong one. I knew I had to turn left at the post box, they've moved it I thought. Went to the top of the road turned and drove back slowly looking for the road I needed; then repeat the performance. All the time I was doing this Nutty was pacing up and down on the back seat, whingeing loudly and voicing his doggy talk, when I looked out to the left he was looking right and vice versa. I then realised what I had done, returned to the traffic lights and took the next turning, Nutty was content, he sat down quietly having put me on the right route. He has done this on other journeys too, although he appears to be sleeping he is aware of the movement of the car and the direction we take and he always pops up to watch the final part of the journey and give his little noises of approval as each turn is taken. Walks with Nutty are never boring; he takes such delight in everything we see. We both enjoy being out in the fresh air and watching the changing seasons. Rain, snow or gales we are out there. One year a pair of Coots raised a family in the dyke beside the road we walked on, Nutty was fascinated by the chicks, they looked like tiny black pom-poms rolling around. Every day when we went out he would firmly march me over to the dyke and we would stand and watch them. I even caught him staring at a broken black brush head someone had left beside the road! As the chicks got bigger and "grew legs" to move around on he lost interest in them. He loved to chase ducks, but never when they had young ones, I just had to tell him No and he would leave them alone.

He enjoys water, crashing about in the reeds flushing out the ducks and gathering up the rubbish. His first introduction to water was not good. As a puppy when we went down the lane at night he would race up the field on the other side of the hedge, U-turn at the top and race back down the road to meet me. The U-turns at the end of the hedge got wider and I could foresee what might happen and it did! He fell into the dyke on the opposite side of the road. I could not see this in the gathering dusk; but I heard it and kept calling him to me. He came back to me cold and wet and then grumbled and whinged all the way home. On another occasion when the family were all together, we went down the marshes at seas end. At high tide the sea leaves deep pools and Freddie was off like a rocket heading for the water, Nutty chased after him but instead of following into the water he put the brakes on just before getting there and slithered along on his bottom in the slimy mud. Deciding this was a more attractive option than getting wet he put his neck down and slithered and rolled in it; everyone else was laughing and although it made me smile I was conscious of the fact that we had travelled in my car. Nothing would persuade him into the water to wash it off, but fortunately I always had a stock of old towels in the boot, I got rid of most of the wet mud but could do nothing about the stench; we took that home with us.

His first experience of a bath followed this event, he was not too keen on this but it was the first of many. This rolling in stinky things seems to be attractive to dogs especially Labradors and was frequently repeated, anything from dead fish, excrement to slimy bird droppings became the desired perfume for the day much to my displeasure. Gradually I am pleased to say, he came to associate this action with a bath so he resisted the urge to do it. Water he likes but baths are only just tolerated.

Nutty likes children but can be a bit jealous if they are in our house and getting too much attention. He is not allowed to play with toys belonging to infants so he will go off and steal a soft teddy that sits on the chair in my bedroom, that he is not allowed to have, and comes parading it proudly before us as if he is saying, look what I've got, just to get some attention diverted to him. He is very concerned if the baby cries and has a very anxious look until the problem is sorted. Likewise with adults who are upset, he is very concerned and will try to get onto their knee to comfort them. As a young puppy he visited Sue and John frequently as I used to do some teaching in their care home and when I worked late they would puppy sit for me. When they looked after him for me John had a snooze in the office every afternoon, Nutty sprawled out on his chest, I believe there were occasions he even shared the bed with John, something I would certainly have disapproved of had I known at the time. After John died Nutty was "shared" with Sue who began to look after him if I had to go away, so our lives became much entwined and we share many memories of his demeanours and antics.

Nutty does not like me making a noise or acting the fool; once when a friend stayed with me for a few days we were listening to Last Night at the Proms, the radio was on loud and we were both giving a robust rendering of "Rule Britannia," with Union Jack hats on our head whilst conducting out invisible orchestra. Nutty removed himself to the far side of the room and lay staring intently; suddenly he flashed over and grabbed my hat, took it and lay on it! That only resulted in peals of laughter and more merriment; he *continued to show his displeasure and would not come near us all evening. But that is enough from me, back to the central subject of this book.*

Chapter 8

*T*ime is passing and I am growing up, but still there are new events to fill the time. I face each day with courage and expectation and in the knowledge that some new experience might come my way. When we all go out together with the bicycles in the evenings we often see other dogs on a lead running sedately alongside the owner on a bike. We watch with interest and do our best not to distract their attention from the owner. One sunny day the mistress thought to try this. We walked from the house to the country lane and there she let me forage in the grass and pick up communications from other dogs that had been there before me; when she thought I had passed sufficient time and had made myself comfortable she put me back on the lead, got on the bike and with an encouraging word to me, she pedalled forward. We were off at a cracking good speed down the lane, legs pumping and stretching, tail streaming out behind and ears flapping in the breeze, what fun! No time to look at what we passed or investigate the grass verge we kept up our pace; all went well until I decided to stop for a wee. I stopped, the bike stopped, SHE carried on over the handlebars and ended up in a crumpled heap on the road with the cycle op top of her. She lay in the road, hurt and winded then screamed at me,

"You stupid dog!"

What had I done? Clearly she was blaming me but I had only stopped to attend to an urgent call of nature and this surely was the purpose of doggy walks, I felt quite bewildered and quite indignant by this attack. She did eventually calm down and had the grace to give me a cuddle and tell me it was not my fault. We made our way slowly and painfully home, pushing the bike, she limped about for a week with plasters on her knees and elbows and painful bruises in places we will not mention here. We did not repeat this exercise. SHE is packing again.

Chapter 9

*N*utty is on a sabbatical he is staying with me for a few days. I love having him and think it a great honour to be trusted with him. I take my responsibilities very seriously and put myself at his disposal working my other chores around his routine. I am fearful of anything happening to him during his stay with me; I never let him off the lead and carry the phone number of the vet in my purse. He is checked over very carefully each day and groomed to within an inch of his life. I am very proud of him when we go for our perambulations for he is much admired and stroked. Both being early risers and both liking to go to bed at a reasonable hour we are complementary to each others needs.

We take our last constitutional of the day about nine and are in bed before ten, so this is what I expected as we set off on our usual evening stroll. We ambled along our chosen route past the railings behind which there is a pond. Nutty stops to eye up his feathered friends and then we are on our *way. We return by a circular route that brings us down to the edge of the pond. As is his way, Nutty is investigating every tree and bush absorbing the smells of all those who have previously passed along this route. The lead is looped around my wrist but hangs loosely from my hand as I day dream, idling the time until he feels he has finished gathering up all the information he needs. Suddenly I am pulled forward at speed. He is in the middle of the pond and I am up to my knees in green algae. I grab a low hanging branch with my free arm and hang grimly on to stop from falling. With difficulty I haul him back and we regain dry land. He is covered in slime and I am likewise. We head for home, squelching as we go, giving much amusement to the local plebs! The journey home is taken up with frantic thoughts of how I am going to get him clean, I know I cannot lift him into the bath and I wouldn't even consider the hose pipe, much too cold for my precious boy.*

I open the garage first, find a large dust sheet and wrap him in this, then I remove my shoes and trousers (good job the back garden is enclosed!) these I drop in the dustbin. I threaten and beg him to "Stay there" whilst I go in and get myself decent, and then I fetch some large containers from the garage and fill them with warm water. Many bucketsful and one full bottle of baby shampoo are used and two hours later I am satisfied that I have done my best. We go in and I have my bath; it is midnight when we get to bed.

I have a very sensitive nose and next morning I awoke to an aroma, I checked, it wasn't me or the house, it was him. I rang the Pet Parlour and explained my problem; I didn't dare return him to his mistress smelling of "Fleur de pond!" and an appointment was made. He was greeted with exclamations of "Bless him" and "Poor boy" and there was much hilarity from the staff as they went to work on him. I sat in the waiting room feeling very neglectful whilst he was restored to his pristine condition.

I am still convinced that he had a smirk on his face on our way home; he was much admired for his gleaming coat. This incident was the first of many and certainly the first time I found out he likes to chase the ducks. We give the pond a wide berth now and I allow him only to peer through the railings at his feathered friends.

I well remember the first time he came to stay; his mistress was going away for just one night and was anxious to find new kennels for him as she had grown unhappy about the one previously used, there being some management problems and Nutty had been stressed on his return, she felt there was something not right.

"Let me have him" I said.

After much discussion this was agreed, so he came over in the afternoon with bed and baggage. I was instructed as to his night routine and told to put him in the conservatory as this was where he slept at home. We had our evening walk and I settled him down in the conservatory with a bedtime biscuit. I was just settled down in bed for a good read when the most ear-splitting howl rent the air. Jumping out of bed I went and soothed him until the worried frown disappeared and thinking that he was settled went back to bed. The howl was repeated, so I brought his blanket into the hall and put it just outside my bedroom door; this settled him.

The next time he came to stay I put the blanket down by the bedroom door in preparation for the night, he looked at me, looked at the blanket and proceeded to drag the blanket into the bedroom, collected his soft toy and sat down firmly on the blanket. He now sleeps always by my bed and wakes me up early by dropping a shoe on my head or pushing an inquisitive cold nose in my face.

I love having Nutty and when my grandchildren come to stay, they spend hours playing with him. My granddaughter grooms him and one day after giving him a thorough brush, cleaned his teeth and polished his nails she looked up to see the rain and was quite put out that he now needed a walk and all her good work was for nothing. Being new to my area Nutty is much admired when we are out, he is such a handsome dog he is patted and stroked by many. One day we stopped to talk to a lady with a pushchair, conversation finished we moved off and we had walked several yards when looking down I saw that he was clutching in his jaws a fluffy white bunny he had filched from the push chair! We chased after the lady but she was so amused by the incident she told him to keep it.

Nutty loves soft toys and scatters them all around the house when he is here. On answering the door to a "cold caller" Looking and feeling irritable at his pushy talk I was trying politely to get rid of him when he looked down and saw Nutty who had come to investigate with a pink pig in his mouth. Laughing out loud he remarked how silly he looked; very carefully I tucked my fingers into Nutty's collar and replied,

"We give him soft toys to hold on the advice of the animal behaviourist because of his erratic behaviour with strangers and his tendency to bite"

Backing off up the drive he said how sorry he was not to be able to help me! I shut the door firmly and felt quite guilty at maligning Nutty's character so I gave him a hug and a small treat. Having seen off the undesirable visitor he returned to snoozing in the back yard whilst keeping an eye open on the cheeky blackbirds that invade his patch. Life is never boring when Nutty is here.

Chapter 10

A poem by Nutty; for Auntie Sue

Can I have a biscuit?

If you would be so kind,

You chose one from out the tin

Any sort I really do not mind.

This is just a little one

Can I have another?

After all you always give

Two biscuits to my mother!

I need to be rewarded

For I'm very kind to you

I share my hairs and all my toys

Even my muddy paws with you.

I take you out for nice wet walks

And get you out of bed.

I keep you on your toes all day

Make sure that I get fed.

So can I have a biscuit?

The vet says I'm getting thinner

So please another biscuit

To put me on till dinner!

As your companion I let you stop and talk

To all our friends we meet upon our walk.

So keep the biscuits handy, they are all for me

You can have your own sort, with a cup of tea.

Can I have a biscuit? I promise I won't tell

She's gone to foreign parts, as you know well.

So she's left me here to care for you

Give me another please, dear Aunty Sue!

*S*o here I am at Sue's I have been told that SHE has gone to Prague so I will pass away the time by telling you more about my life story. My mistress is very proud of me and we have had some good times together, we go on lovely walks and spent our days together. I like my walks with Auntie Sue as well as there are new places to visit and new people to fuss me. Her friends want to pat me and make a fuss of me, they have not seen a chocolate coloured Labrador before and were impressed by my looks. I was told I had a noble head, but I knew that anyway. Sue is careful about my person and keeps me well groomed, brushing until my coat is gleaming and cleaning my ears and teeth. At home although I am groomed sad to say the mistress is not always quite as particular, but I still look good. The more I was admired the prouder Sue got, no wonder I became conceited. I liked best our walks by the river, there was so much to see and do and I enjoyed chasing the ducks, what a noise they made as I scattered them and sent them into the water! I soon learnt to swim so I could follow them, I would take a flying leap and land far out in the river; people were amazed at my diving and would stand and watch me showing off and it was fun shaking water all over everyone when I climbed out. One day leaping into the water near the bridge I landed near a large Pike that was quietly sunning itself, it got a rude awakening, leaping three feet in the air before shooting off up the river.

SHE is back. Back from this place called Prague. They have had lunch together and I have treated HER with cool disdain, sticking close to Sue just to show my displeasure. I have heard them plotting to repeat this arrangement (they seem to think I don't understand this conversation.) Actually my stay here has been good, a vast improvement on kennels. I was able to have my blanket next to her bed and this arrangement suited us both, she was not disturbed in the night and I was able to get her up early in the morning by washing her face. Sue believes that a dog should receive walks on demand even if it is only five in the morning, and is not averse to slipping me a titbit when I look forlorn. Whenever I am away from home I insist on sleeping next to the bed even if the mistress is with me; I feel more secure and am able to keep guard on the door to ensure whoever is there, they can't sneak off without me. Members of Sue's family have made special visits to see me, and the Grandchildren have argued over who should brush my coat, clean my teeth and feed me. They also like to roll about on the floor for some games and face washing and ear licking sessions. This is how it should be and I give hearty approval to this regime.

Back home I find that in my absence my conservatory has gone! I now sleep in the kitchen but this is a temporary arrangement for soon the workmen arrive and erect a new one, I have a roof over my head again and a very smart room which is to be my domain complete with central heating, however there is a new arrangement for exiting this new conservatory. So that the door can be kept closed there is a special opening for me; my own private little door. I am being taught to use the dog flap, what next! I am reluctant to subject myself to the humiliation of not knowing how to do it. I am being coaxed to go through this hole with biscuits. Me on one side and the biscuit on the other, what a dilemma! My cries of concern and distress are ignored as she watches me through the window and calls me. When I experiment with a little push the flap snaps back and hits me on the nose, I jump back startled, then after several tries I am shoved through from behind! This attack on my person is a great affront to my dignity! Mistress is muttering something about bringing in the local cat fraternity to show me how to do it! This process is repeated many times and I am learning, slowly. This evening my dinner was put outside the flap, I soon had myself through it but was very reluctant to get back inside through this hole and whined whilst she looked at me through the window and tried to coax me back. I fear it will be some time before I feel at ease with this arrangement. Now that we have this new arrangement my outside kennel and pen have become redundant they have been taken away and Freddie and Fly now have the pleasure of them. My mistress has been spending much time in the garden just lately (so has friend Sue) this must be due to the time of the year. Why is it that they are allowed to dig and when I do it I am scolded? Why are they allowed to plant things in tubs yet when I bury my bone in one, this brings frowns of disapproval and I am accused of being a vandal? I am a good gardener. I remember one day when I was very young and visiting Sue and John I found some tea bags in the garden so being helpful I gathered them up and brought them in.

John removed them and put them around the roots of his plants, I retrieved them and gave him them back. He then went out and buried them but I was watching; I dug them up and brought them back! They were very muddy; I was very fond of Uncle John we go back a long way. When I was small I used to curl up on his chest and we would both have a well-deserved siesta. He never minded when I washed his face but when I was very, very small and had only just met him, I disgraced myself by piddling all down him when he picked me up! I have never been allowed to forget this embarrassing moment, and neither was he! Speaking of forgetfulness, I have noticed that both the mistress and Auntie Sue are getting absent minded, or they lack concentration for they are always losing things. When we go to the car, the mistress invariably has to return to the house for something. She is constantly demanding of me, where are the keys? We both have to rush frantically around the house to find them. If only she would hang them on the hook when she came in instead of dumping them, we would not get this delay at the beginning of every outing. I don't know why she expects me to find them I can't; I just rush around looking intelligent until she locates them. I must not complain neither of them has actually forgotten to walk me or feed me, not that they would get away with it if they tried. I am adept at making my wants known and can be persistent and insistent when the need arises. Mind you we can all be a bit absentminded; I took a drink from the water feature the other day, forgetting that I was carrying one of the mistresses slippers around, it went for a swim and mistress had to fish it out, not very pleased to have a soggy slipper. (This water feature is only a pretentious name used by mistress for a barrel of water on the patio, but it satisfies her vanity and provides me with another source of refreshment.)

At last, there is some floor covering in the conservatory; I am no longer sleeping in a bare cell. A table and comfortable chair have appeared so it looks as if mistress is intending spending more time here with me. These changes, including all these jaunts, seem to have come about since she retired from work, I approve of this if it means more time for me. She is talking of going off again; next time she has a bath (I usually go in to see that she is alright and take a sneaky lick at the soap) I will give her a sneaky look over for I think she must be growing wings. Still, she seems to have more time at home and more time for walks, so that is a bonus.

The autumn is drawing to a close, the night falls early and gets very cold, but during the day when the sun is shining it is still warm enough to snooze in the garden, which I do plenty of. We like to walk through the woods where the ground is now carpeted with leaves that scrunch underfoot. I snuffle deep into the piles of leaves, there are lots of little creatures and insects buried in them; we play hide and seek. The horses we see in the fields all have their blankets on to keep them warm. The mistress bought me a coat once presumably worried about me catching cold; I rolled over and over and shook myself vigorously in my efforts to get it off so the walk did not progress very well. I think she got the message that I didn't like wearing it and it got relegated to the back of the cupboard. These dark evenings once the curtains are drawn she doesn't seem to be so active, I lie on my blanket at her feet whilst she reads and it is all very cosy and peaceful.

What a surprise waited for us when we emerged this morning the ground is covered in a soft blanket. Snow she tells me. I like it! It is cold and wet; I roll in it, slide my neck in it, eat it and race around for sheer joy at this new experience. She picks it up and makes balls from it then throws them for me but when they fall to the floor they just disappear. All the way down the lane I revel in this magic snuff, racing across the fields in sheer delight. Some of my friends with long hair don't like it as it sticks to their paws making them cold and uncomfortable but I like the cold and always feel more alert and energetic in the winter months, so this snow is wonderful. When we return the children are all outside rolling up great balls of this snow and putting hats on top of them and being pulled about on a sledge; they are all very excited, shouting and laughing and looking rosy cheeked. I join in, racing and sliding and rolling over in ecstasy. The adults too are outside watching with steaming mugs held in their hands; it is all very friendly and jolly. The snow stayed around all week so my pleasure in it was an extended one.

Chapter 11

$\mathcal{L}$ife has been quite eventful since I last recorded some of my memoirs so I thought it was time I wrote down a few things to put the record to rights. The Mistress has been busy decorating turning the house upside down so I am left to my own devices and have had time to mull over the past and the meaning of life. I have recalled memories from the past and analysed present events which are giving me some concern, so I will now set them out before you and let you be the judge about the rightness of these words.

As I have said, the Mistress has been decorating, whilst not exactly ignoring my needs I most certainly was not the main consideration, the attention she paid me was definitely lacking in both quality and quantity; well except for being chased from pillar to post when I got in her way. I have been observing her behaviour and noting that it seems to be an unfair world. When

I do things wrong there is always someone present to moan about it but this is not so for her, she gets away with things. She has not been happy with the way things were progressing in the bathroom, there has been much sighing and muttering and humping too and fro. She even rang Auntie Sue and groused to her about the behaviour of the paint and paper! In fact I reckon the Mistress was having a mega sulk, but did anyone comment on this? No! Did I raise my voice in rebuke when she stepped off the ladder into the paint tray? Did I say anything when she threw her damp cloth into the bucket of water and missed and it went into the tin of paint? No! Did anyone criticise the loud angry words used when balancing on the rim of the toilet she slipped and fell, hitting her painful wrist on the side of the bath? No! I kept silent as I say, it is an unfair world. The Mistress was also into swatting flies to keep them off the paint; she has an instrument to use for this and it gives quite a thwack. I am sorry for the flies and I am never quite sure if that thing will come my way so I cringe and beat my tail, keeping well out of the way whenever she uses it.

Normally one of my favourite spots when she is working at home is in front of the hall radiator it is warm and comforting and I can see in most directions and keep an eye on what she is up to. I lie here quietly whilst she works on the computer and jump up when I hear the little bleep noise the computer makes when she logs off; now it is ME time. She has never objected to me being in this spot, but today this place by the radiator appears to be out of bounds; I keep getting moved on with impatient words and much muttering and even a shove from a foot. There are deep sighs and moans when she discovers the radiator covered in dark hairs, and of course I got the blame. But consider was I doing anything that I did not normally do? I was not! Had anyone taken the trouble to explain to me that paint was antisocial sticky stuff that I should avoid? They had not! Was I told that paint sneaks up behind you and steals the hairs off your back? I was not! So you judge for yourself, was I to blame? I have been having a closer look at her tools and discover she uses brushes filled with dark hairs; If this crime had been properly investigated I am convinced that forensic tests would demonstrate my innocence in this matter, as I shall now go on to show to you my innocence in yet another area where I, the innocent one, got the blame. Just lately the Mistress has seen piles of earth in the flowerbeds and the cry goes up,

"Have you been digging?"

But right triumphs in the end, she has got her comeuppance; the perpetrator of the crime has shown his hand by tunnelling under the lawn and leaving piles of earth. Yes you have it, we have a mole! She used to laugh at Uncle John when he had a mole in his garden, so now it serves her right. Has she apologised? Not a bit of it, she has probably forgotten that she has been blaming me, but I don't forget. I keep silent but I store it all up, my time will come. It is no wonder that some dogs have psychiatric problems when treated by their owners like this. Not that I have, but I understand that Sue has relatives with a dog who has been diagnosed by the vet to be psychotic. Probably the owners fault, really these humans just do not understand what makes a dog tick and are not consistent in their dealings with us.

They do not understand the trauma caused by them going away and leaving us. I have been left twice recently. Once with Auntie Sue whilst SHE went off to London to go on the Eye; what nonsense! Still I was able to boss Sue around, slept in her room and got her up at five by dropping a plimsoll on her head. That soon got her out for an early walk. A chap likes to be powerful. Later the same week she was off to London again to see a show. She had the audacity to get me up far too early to take me for a walk before she went off to catch the bus. At least she had made arrangements with my good neighbours to take me out again and feed me; so I had the family for company and had a play with Daisy in the fields. (She is another dog with psychiatric problems in my opinion) Midnight when SHE came back with the excuse that the bus had broken down, she had to wake me up for my bedtime drink.

The son Pete has been home so I have had lots of walks down the river. I showed Pete how I can get in and out of my new hatch, which I do with ease despite all the rude comments made about my girth.

I quite like this now as it gives me more freedom and I am not dependant on HER. The other night whilst she was attending to my bedtime needs, the phone rang and she went off to talk to someone. I do not like my routine interrupted, so I asked to be let out the backdoor, went round the corner, through the hatch and put myself to bed. She had to come looking for me as she was waiting in the kitchen to let me back in. The new conservatory is cosy and warm and I am well pleased with it. The Mistress joins me there and we have a quiet hour together basking in the warmth even when it is a bit cold and wet outside.

I believe that SHE is planning an extended trip sometime this month and I am going to stay with Sue. When will she realise that a woman's place is in the home? Good job Sue knows her place or where would I be? I am sure you will agree when you have read this that I am a much maligned dog. I think that we dogs should get together to share our grievances. I have heard tell of a special organisation that has our particular welfare at heart and will give us protection, but no one wants to tell us about it. All we get by way of support is trips to the vet and they only listen to what the owners say.

Chapter 12

$\mathcal{A}$t various times of his life Nutty has visited the vet for vaccinations checkups, sometimes because he is ill and of course for his operations. He goes eagerly and is always well behaved and suffers any form of interference silently but is quick out of the door as soon as it opens, taking the lead in his mouth and tugging urgently. When he was young he was always very good at taking medication; prize open the jaws, drop in pill, hold jaws shut, pill gone, but not anymore. As he has got older he seems to object to taking pills, struggles and resists any attempt to insert one in his mouth, so I have had to resort to subterfuge. I first try the standard method, when this does not work, the pill is carefully hidden in a piece of buttered bread and given to him; he takes it then spits it out. I have never seen a dog spit before but he really does, the morsel is projected a couple of feet. Retrieve the pill, make another sandwich with peanut butter which he likes I give it to him; he spits. Losing patience I cram the pill down his *throat; it's gone or so I think. I give him a little milky drink to wash it down and whilst he is lapping that I gather up the bread and go out to throw it to the birds. I pass Nutty on the way back, I find the dissolved pill floating on top of the dregs of the milk; he is now outside eating the bread.*

Because of his arthritis he is given supplements such as fish oils and special dietary food to keep him active and well. Everything possible is purchased and tried, any new food or potion is purchased to keep him in pristine condition; in fact he has better health care than I have but these efforts have not been in vain for Nutty is still a bouncy dog who in spite of advancing years still things he is a puppy.

Chapter 13

I am always wary when there is a suitcase in evidence followed by a trip to Auntie Sue's; am I being left or is she coming too? We all three set off on one of our many adventures. It seems a long journey and I stretch out on the back seat and catch up with some serious sleep. Breaking the journey for a pit stop, first one then the other disappears into the building and emerges with a smile on the face and a coffee in the fist. I am left with the one on the outside and watch anxiously for the return of both. I refuse to go for my necessary walk until the mistress is back. Once we are all comfortable we head off again and eventually reach our destination. These have been quite varied. I particularly remember the cottage in Oswestry; it had a very handy park opposite it which was a good area for me to explore each day. They had a bedroom each and I slept with the mistress (but on the floor) in the morning I went from room to room to peer at each of them in turn to see which off them I could rouse first. I rest my head on the bed and stare deep into the depths of their sluggish brain with my hypnotic powers to see which eye I could force open first, once that was done I had their attention. It was usually my owner who made the effort to take me out and Sue would have the breakfast on by the time we got back. Plans were then made for the day; many of the outings took us past the forest and we always stopped to do some serious exploring here. I like it; space and smells and smells and more smells. Head down and tail up I would follow the trail of rabbit, deer and many more not seen but whose presence I felt. There were lots of holes to sniff into and wonder what lived in them. I gave chase to any that had the temerity to cross my path but never succeeded in bringing them down.

On one such trip out we went on a boat up the river, the barge was pulled by a horse so it was a slow ride. We had to wait because the Blacksmith was putting new shoes on the horse, so we whiled away the time watching the wild fowl on the water. After the trip we wandered through the small town and eventually came to the river, it was fast flowing, cascading and bouncing over stones and creating a thunderous noise. There were lots of families picnicking on the bank and small boys throwing sticks into the water. Of course I went in; it wasn't too deep so I stood out in the middle of the water waiting in anticipation for them to throw me a ball. They kept trying to coax me out but I ignored this, it was my holiday after all. I was enjoying the feel of the icy water pulsing against my body, tugging, and pushing me, it was invigorating, but I didn't realise the current was moving me closer to the edge of a cascading waterfall until with a great swoosh my feet could find no substance and I was falling. The water hurled and tumbled me around until I landed in a turbulent pool at the bottom with water gushing on top of me forcing me down into the depths. I struck out and getting my bearings swam to the edge and scrambled out and gave myself a good shake over all those standing on the bank still with open-mouthed horror displayed on their faces. I was then taken into the nearby woods away from the water, which was just as full of fun for me but certainly much less fraught for them.

We have had great holidays in Yorkshire for there are plenty of rivers, plenty of open spaces and woods to explore and lots of things to chase. Also boring trips into town where I had to be held on a lead outside as they took it in turns to browse, whoever had me I would fix my eyes on the shop door and refuse to move and did a bit of whingeing as well until I persuaded them back out. Nevertheless they still managed to be laden down with interesting packages which we would all explore once we got back to our holiday let. We spent one day in the lake district, an absolute washout that was. We arrived in torrential rain and sat for hours in the car waiting for it to abate. Eventually SHE decided that I needed to get out for a comfort stop, struggling into a raincoat she gets out, opens the back door and fastens my lead on then tries to coax me from the car, in this rain? Not a chance, I thought and resisted the tugs, she put her knee onto the edge of the seat and pulled with all her might, but I was not to be moved. Sue was laughing, the mistress muttering about the RSPA notice at the car park entrance about being prosecuted for leaving dogs in cars, but I would not budge. Eventually they both went out in the rain pretending they were enjoying themselves; I stayed warm and dry in the comfort of the back seat. Then there were the trips to the caravan, this was not my favourite place as it was at the top of a hill and with my arthritis it became a problem for me. One of our relatives has a barge so when we visit there we have been out on water trips, the mistress will ask for us to be put ashore and we walk along the canal bank then get picked up further along. If it is the right time of the year she will pick blackberries and will feed me the occasional one. She even slept on the floor with me, very cosy, but she wouldn't do this at home. Wherever we go the navigation is usually a problem when the mistress is driving, we always get lost. Auntie Sue is supposed to be the navigator but is hopeless at map reading and can't see the road signs without her glasses which through stubborn pride she refuses to wear. When there is a choice to be made there is much discussion in the front of the car and a lot of giggles as they discus the options; eventually we set off again but are they on the right route I wonder? If I had been there before I would recognise where we went astray and would pace anxiously on the back seat and whinge until they got themselves on the right route. I mostly slept on long journeys but as we neared our destination I would perk up, peer out the windscreen between the two of them and give an approving little murmur in the back of my throat as we took the correct turns. I do have my uses.

Chapter 14

I feel that I am now coming to the end of my story which I hope you have enjoyed; I have led a very varied life and enjoyed it but I don't want to bore you with too many tales. I have been fortunate to have a comfortable home and a devoted mistress (with back up from Auntie Sue.) My life has been interesting; I have made my mark and become a special feature in the area. I am told that as I get older I am growing into a grumpy old man, but this is not so, I just feel that in deference to my age she should be a bit quicker off the starting block when I want something. On the whole we rub along together quite well with each other and who knows what new experiences still lie in wait? I am satisfied with my life, I have walked this path quietly and peacefully, a good companion and a friend to all. I have faced every new day with enthusiasm and courage, and now in the twilight of my years all

I want is to be at home with my special person and enjoy our somewhat slower forages down the lane. We do not stray far from home now but I am always eager to get out and to meet new friends, both human and canine, so if one day our paths should cross, stop and say hello; I am sure you will agree that I am a very fine dog indeed.

Nutty came into my life when he was eight weeks old and I was newly widowed and thought to have a dog for company. I loved him from the time of setting eyes on him but there were times when I stood and looked at the devastation he caused that I wondered what I had done! But his enthusiasm for life, boundless energy, and the unconditional love he gave to me made it all worthwhile. He has brought much joy into my life and been popular with family and friends. Nutty is getting old now with all the problems related to age, his hearing is less acute, he has cataracts and his back legs are failing so he has to sit down often but he still loves his walks though we do not go as far and amble rather than stride out. Meeting other dogs he can still summons the energy to make a token gesture towards playing, his zest for life is unabated. He made me go out and meet people and through him I have made new friends. He has brought me joy and much laughter. He knows my every mood and when I am feeling blue he is anxious and comes to comfort me. When I am ill and perhaps spend a day in bed he is content to amuse himself just coming to check on me from time to time and give me a little lick so that I know that the "nurse" has visited.

He resembles a large brown bear and has been my faithful companion, protective in his way but really he is a big gentle giant; large enough to keep strangers at a distance, soft enough to attract all the neighbouring children. Nutty is a fun dog; great to be with, devious at times but very entertaining. He is very intelligent and despite the experience of puppy classes, he learns fast; I never really had to train him, just gave a command and he did it, I didn't need him to perform tricks. He is a great pet and I am sure he would have made an excellent assistance dog. When I first took him out in the dark and let him off the lead I would stare into the dark calling him back wondering where he was, it took me a while to realise he had never left my side yet in daytime he would be off. Similarly when I put the lights off in the house, he guides me forward seeming to know I can't see as well as him in the dark. One thing that has not changed with the years are his eyes, they are still deep pools of mystery.

Anyone who owns a dog will know the work they cause, time consuming costly visits to the vet, walks in all weathers, grooming and of course the daily vacuuming that is necessary to get rid of liberally distributed hairs. Nutty is brushed daily even so he sheds enough hair to staff a cushion; I have at times threatened to spray him with liquid glue! So if you are not prepared to spend time with them, giving the care they need, enjoying their company and to take the rough with the smooth, don't get a dog, a dog is a commitment, but the benefits far outweigh the drawbacks, it is wonderful to come home to a friendly presence and a warm welcome. Unlike humans, dogs are never moody; they will always be pleased to see you even if you were a bit grumpy with them when you left them. Nutty has always hated being abandoned; on the odd occasion I have tied him up outside a shop, even though he can see me through the door, he howls and whines. Even if he is left outside a shop with Sue he is never happy until I take over the holding of the lead; we are glued together for life. What the future holds I know not, hopefully despite his age he will still be with me for some time yet, but whatever time he has left, nothing can take away the past; both Sue and I get much pleasure from recalling his misdeeds and funny antics. For now we settle for our quieter routine and many hours sleeping at my feet. There are still funny little incidents that happen with him not quite as dramatic as those in the past but still funny enough to raise a smile. Sue and I never tire of reminiscing about our shared experiences of Nutty and both of us enjoy his company and are aware of the great benefit he has brought to our advancing years. We grow old together. When the time comes to part with him he will be sorely missed but never forgotten: his name is engraved upon my heart.

Lightning Source UK Ltd.
Milton Keynes UK
02 February 2011

166782UK00001B/24/P

9 781449 083939